Kate Middleton

By Petrice Custance

CRABTREE
Publishing Company
www.crabtreebooks.com

CRABTREE
PUBLISHING COMPANY
WWW.CRABTREEBOOKS.COM

Dedicated by Petrice Custance
To my parents, Sid and Joni Custance, with much love

Author: Petrice Custance

Editor: Crystal Sikkens

Proofreader: Lorna Notsch

Photo research: Crystal Sikkens, Ken Wright

Design and prepress: Ken Wright

Print coordinator: Katherine Berti

Photo Credits

Alamy: title page, Feature Eye Image
AP Images: p 5, Frank Augstein; p 11, TOBY MELVILLE; p 13, MICHAEL PROBST; p 17, ITV/PA Wire URN:9789826 (Press Association via AP Images)
Getty: p 15, Tim Graham; p 18, KIRSTY WIGGLESWORTH; p 20, George Pimentel; p 21, WPA Pool; p 25, AFP Contributor; p 27, The White House / Handout; p 28, Chris Jackson;
iStock: p 19 (bottom), coldsnowstorm

Keystone: pp 6, 9, ©ZUMApress.com; pp 7, 8, © FAME Pictures; p 12, Photo by PALMER/MIILAN/BIG Pictures UK/KEYSTONE Press. (©) Copyright 2006 by BIG Pictures UK; p 14, Photo by Rebecca Reid/Pressnet/KEYSTONE Press. (©) Copyright 2005 by Pressnet; p 23, Photo by Mario Testino / AdMedia/KEYSTONE Press © Copyright 2015 by AdMedia; p 24, © wenn.com/wenn.com; p 26, Keystone Press via ZUMA Press;
Shutterstock: pp 4, 22, Featureflash Photo Agency; p 10 (top), Simona Bottone; p 10 (bottom), Pamela Loreto Perez; p 19 (top), Dutourdumonde Photography
Shutterstock Premier: p 16, ©Alan Davidson/Silverhub/REX/Shutterstock; p 28 (left), ©Tim Rooke/REX/Shutterstock
Wikimedia: p 29, Sodacan

NOTE: Images on page 7 www.officialroyalwedding2011.org

Every effort has been made to trace copyright holders and to obtain their permission for use of copyright material. The authors and publishers would be pleased to rectify any error or omission in future editions. All the Internet addresses given in this book were correct at the time of going to press. The author and publishers regret any inconvenience caused if addresses have changed or sites have ceased to exist, but can accept no responsibility for any such changes.

Library and Archives Canada Cataloguing in Publication

Custance, Petrice, author
      Kate Middleton / Petrice Custance.

(Superstars!)
Includes index.
Issued in print and electronic formats.
ISBN 978-0-7787-4831-1 (hardcover).--
ISBN 978-0-7787-4846-5 (softcover).--
ISBN 978-1-4271-2094-6 (HTML)

      1. Catherine, Duchess of Cambridge, 1982- --Juvenile literature. 2. Princesses--Great Britain--Biography--Juvenile literature. I. Title. II. Series: Superstars! (St. Catharines, Ont.)

DA591.A45W5556 2018   j941.086'12092   C2018-900274-3
                                             C2018-900275-1

Library of Congress Cataloging-in-Publication Data

CIP available at the Library of Congress

Crabtree Publishing Company

www.crabtreebooks.com   1-800-387-7650

Printed in the U.S.A./052018/BG20180327

Published in Canada
Crabtree Publishing
616 Welland Ave.
St. Catharines, ON
L2M 5V6

Published in the United States
Crabtree Publishing
PMB 59051
350 Fifth Avenue, 59th Floor
New York, New York 10118

Published in the United Kingdom
Crabtree Publishing
Maritime House
Basin Road North, Hove
BN41 1WR

Published in Australia
Crabtree Publishing
3 Charles Street
Coburg North
VIC 3058

CONTENTS

Words that are defined in the glossary are in
bold type the first time they appear in the text.

Modern Fairy Tale

Kate Middleton is the **descendant** of coal miners, and one day she will become queen of England. Countless fairy tales tell the story of a young woman who marries Prince Charming. But only a small number of people have lived the fairy tale in real life. On April 29, 2011, Kate Middleton joined that small group when she married Prince William, the grandson of the current Queen of England. Now known as the Duchess of Cambridge, Kate represents a new and modern direction for the British royal family. Kate is helping to make "The Firm," as the family is popularly called, more **inclusive** and **relatable** than ever before.

The Duke and Duchess of Cambridge leaving Westminster Abbey in an open carriage following their wedding ceremony

In the Spotlight

Kate is one of the most famous women in the world. She is photographed endlessly, and her every fashion move is obsessed over. Kate employs a stylist to help her look her best when in the public eye. She often wears clothes made by British designers to help **promote** British goods around the world.
Kate wears many of her outfits more than once. This is known as fashion recycling because it is practical and financially responsible.

While Kate enjoys making eye-catching fashion choices, her main focus is on **charity** work. She promotes several charities by shining a global spotlight on them.

Heads Together, a charity started by Kate, William, and his brother, Prince Harry, is dedicated to spreading awareness about the importance of **mental health**.

A Future Queen Is Born

Catherine Elizabeth Middleton was born on January 9, 1982, in Reading, England. Her father, Michael, and mother, Carole, both worked for British Airways when they met. Michael was a **flight dispatcher**, and Carole was a **flight attendant**. Michael comes from a long line of lawyers and wealthy wool merchants. Carole comes from **working-class** roots, including generations of coal miners and construction workers.

Traditionally, British people have not had the opportunity to change their **class**, which was determined by birth. This meant that children entered into the same class as their parents. A person's class determined every aspect of their lives—where they lived and went to school, their job, who they married, etc. The fact that Kate, a "**commoner**," will one day be queen has signaled a major change in ideas about class in Britain.

Michael and Carole Middleton

6

New Adventures

In May 1984, the family, including Kate's baby sister Pippa, moved to Amman, Jordan, in the Middle East. Michael had been offered a job there for two years, and he and Carole viewed the move as an adventurous opportunity for the family. In Jordan, two-year-old Kate attended a **multicultural** preschool. Her classmates were from many different countries around the world. Kate learned a bit of the Arabic language by reading short verses from the **Koran**.

Kate, age three, on a family holiday in the Lake District, England

Kate, age four, with her father and sister Pippa in Jerash, Jordan

7

Happy School Days

In 1986, the family moved back to England. That year, Kate began school at St Andrew's Prep, an expensive private elementary school, paid for by a **trust fund** through her father's family. Kate was known as a slightly shy, well-mannered girl who loved playing sports and climbing trees. Her sports instructor, Denise Allford, described Kate as a "100-mile-per-hour girl." Kate's favorite sport was field hockey. She was also a competitive swimmer and broke many school records. Although shy, Kate loved being on stage and performed in most of her school's theatrical productions. She also loved music. She learned to play the flute and piano, and was also a talented singer.

Party Pieces

In 1987, Carole Middleton began an at-home business called Party Pieces. The mail-order company sells children's party supplies and is now a multimillion-dollar business. Kate and Pippa used to model for the company.

When Kate was five, her younger brother James was born. He is seen here with Pippa.

Difficult Times

In 1995, Kate left St Andrew's Prep for Downe House, a **prestigious** all-girls private school. Most of the students were boarders, which meant they lived at the school during the week. Kate was nervous about attending the school and did not want to be a boarder. Because of this, she had trouble making friends, and it was rumored that she was a victim of teasing and bullying there. Halfway through the year, Kate's parents pulled her out of Downe House and enrolled her at Marlborough College. For a fresh start, Kate decided to be a boarder at Marlborough. She was much happier there, and excelled both academically and at sports, especially field hockey. In her last year at Marlborough, she became a school **ambassador**, and would go to London to different events to promote the school. Kate had blossomed into a confident speaker.

Kate with her friend Gemma Williamson at Marlborough College

Kate and Pippa (back row) with the Marlborough College girls' field hockey team

Away from Home

In the year 2000, Kate decided to take a gap year, a popular trend for British students, when they take a year off to travel and work or volunteer before beginning university. That September, Kate traveled to Florence, Italy, for a three-month program to study the Italian language and art. She loved touring all the galleries and museums and made many friends while there. She also brought along a professional camera, as she had developed an interest in photography and was thinking of it as a potential career. Kate was also an excellent cook, and loved to throw dinner parties with her roommates in Florence.

The Uffizi Gallery in Florence, Italy, is one of the most famous Italian museums. People from all around the world come to see its priceless artworks.

Hard Worker

In January 2001, Kate began a three-month expedition to Chile through a British-based company called Raleigh International. This company coordinates community and environmental projects in South America. While in Chile, Kate taught primary students, helped build a fire station, and conducted a **marine survey** with British and Chilean scientists.

Kate returned to England at the end of March 2001 and took a summer job as a deckhand at the Ocean Village Marina in Southampton. She washed the decks of boats, loaded boxes, packed away sails, performed safety demonstrations, and learned to **heave a line**. She earned $75 a day.

Prince William also attended Raleigh International during his gap year. He completed the same program just days before Kate arrived.

He Said It

"She was a naturally competent person and you could tell she had been sailing before. She had a good head on her shoulders. She was keen to learn and she had the right attitude."
−Cal Tomlinson, Kate's skipper at the Ocean Village Marina, from *Kate: The Future Queen*

Friends First

In September 2001, Kate began studying art history at St Andrews University in Scotland. This was the same school and program that Prince William was enrolled in. She lived in the same dorm as William, called St. Salvator's—she was on the first floor and William was on the second. At school, William asked everyone to call him William Wales. Kate quickly became friends with William, as they had much in common—a love of outdoors, sports, and skiing, they had both experienced the same gap year expedition in Chile, and they were both studying art history. William was a very private person, but he trusted Kate, and she became one of his closest friends.

Team Player

During her years at university, Kate played field hockey, joined many clubs, and had a part-time job serving tables at a bistro in town.

During their university years, William, Kate, and their circle of friends often preferred to host dinner parties instead of going out to pubs, in order to ensure William's privacy.

Romance Blooms

For their second year of school, William did something that once would have been considered shocking. Instead of staying at the dorm, he invited Kate and two other friends to share a house with him. The house was equipped with bulletproof windows and a security system to ensure William's and his housemates' safety. Over time, Kate's relationship with William grew into a romance. In June 2003, Kate's family threw her a belated 21st birthday party at their home, and William attended. The press started to suspect that there was a relationship between William and Kate. And on April 1, 2004, during a skiing holiday in the Swiss Alps, a picture of William gazing at Kate ran on the front page of *The Sun* newspaper. The headline read "Finally…Wills gets a girl." Kate Middleton was about to become a household name.

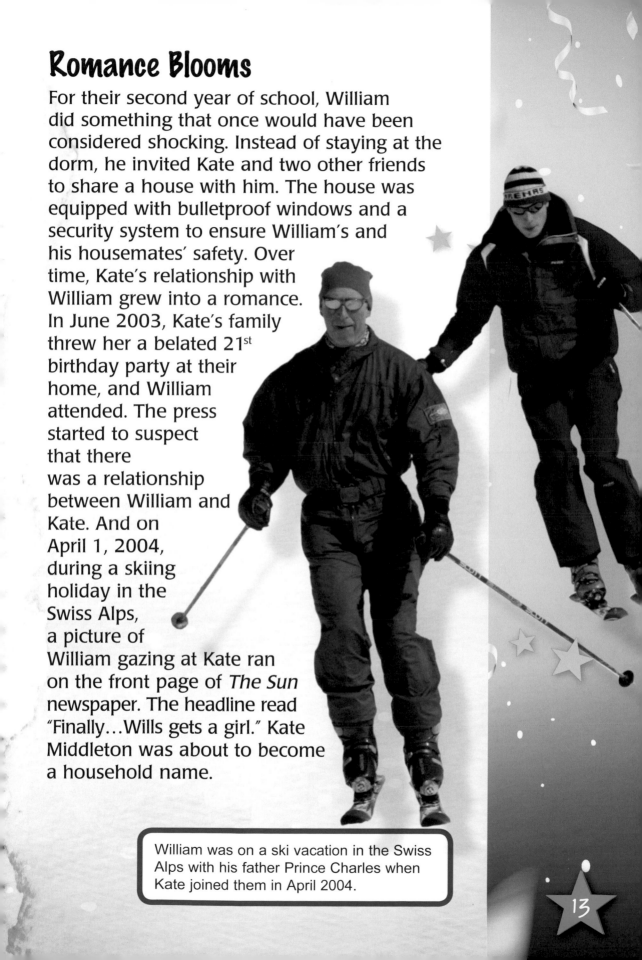

William was on a ski vacation in the Swiss Alps with his father Prince Charles when Kate joined them in April 2004.

13

Life In London

On June 23, 2005, Kate and William graduated from St Andrews. The graduation was attended by the Queen and her husband Prince Philip. Kate moved into an apartment her parents owned in Chelsea, a neighborhood in London. Now with an art history degree, she began submitting her résumé to galleries in London.

Kate was constantly being followed by **paparazzi**. To help her handle the media, Kate received training and guidance from William's press advisers. Kate also experienced cruelty by the press and some members of the British upper classes who felt her background was not suitable for a royal bride. Kate never publicly showed any frustration over this treatment.

Kate during the graduation ceremony at St Andrews University

Time Apart

In 2006, Kate took a job as an accessories buyer for a department store called Jigsaw, and William left London to begin military training. They often saw each other on weekends at her parents' home. William had become quite close with her family. Kate had also been accepted into William's family.

There was much press speculation about when Kate and William would become engaged. It's possible this pressure is what led the couple to break up in April 2007. It is reported that Kate was heartbroken, and that she received supportive messages from Prince Charles and Prince Harry. However, the break-up was short-lived, and by the beginning of June they were back together.

Diana

Kate is often compared to Prince William's mother, Diana, Princess of Wales. In her lifetime, Diana was the most famous woman in the world. She was loved, admired, and photographed endlessly. Diana was tragically killed in a car crash in Paris on August 31, 1997.

Waity Katie

As the years passed, and Kate and William continued to date but with no engagement announcement coming, the press began to nickname Kate "Waity Katie." The press often reported that she didn't seem to have any career ambitions or direction. She had left her job at Jigsaw and didn't seem to be doing much of anything except waiting to see William on weekends. Carole Middleton suggested Kate work for the family business, Party Pieces. Kate updated the website and worked on marketing and promotions, using her photographic skills for the company catalog. Kate also began working with a children's charity called Starlight, which helps children with a serious or terminal disease. She made secret trips to children's hospitals, arranged art workshops for the children, and organized a gala event for the charity. William supported her by attending the gala.

Kate at the 2009 Starlight Gala she helped to organize

The Time Is Right

In October 2010, during a holiday in Kenya, Africa, William proposed to Kate. He had hidden his mother's diamond and sapphire ring in his knapsack. It is said that Kate had no idea he was going to propose. On November 16, 2010, the engagement was officially announced to the press. William and Kate sat together for a televised interview that same evening. It was the first time the world heard Kate speak.

William and Kate during a television interview on the day they announced their engagement

" He Said It "

"It's very special to me. As Kate's very special to me now, it was right to put the two together. It was my way of making sure my mother didn't miss out on today and the excitement and the fact that we are going to spend the rest of our lives together."
—William on giving Kate his mother's ring, in a BBC televised interview, November 16, 2010

Wedding Day

On April 29, 2011, with nearly two billion people watching worldwide, Kate married her Prince Charming. Kate and her father traveled to Westminter Abbey in a glass-roofed Rolls Royce. Cheering crowds lined the route. Her sister Pippa was her maid of honor, and Prince Harry was the best man. Nineteen hundred guests were seated in Westminter Abbey and watched as Kate made her way up the aisle to say "I do." Among the guests were locals from Kate's home village, such as the postman, butcher, and owner of the local pub, as well as celebrities, including David and Victoria Beckham.

Shh!

The designer of Kate's dress was a successfully kept secret—Sarah Burton, the head designer at the British fashion house Alexander McQueen. The dress had a 6.5-foot (2-m) train.

Starry-Eyed

After the ceremony, William and Kate rode to Buckingham Palace in the same open carriage his parents had traveled in on their wedding day. Back at Buckingham Palace, they appeared on the balcony and, in a tradition set by William's parents nearly 30 years before, kissed each other, to the delight of the massive crowd.

That evening, at Buckingham Palace, there was a wedding reception for 300 family and friends. Kate changed into a strapless ivory satin gown with an **angora** jacket. The British singer Ellie Goulding performed during the reception, including her song "Starry Eyed," which was reportedly William and Kate's first dance as husband and wife. The evening ended at about 3 a.m., in the Buckingham Palace gardens, with a huge fireworks display.

On the day of the wedding, it was announced that the Queen had given William and Kate the titles of Duke and Duchess of Cambridge.

Before the reception, William drove Kate from Buckingham Palace to Clarence House in his father's convertible. With all the excitement, he forgot to release the emergency brake!

Working Royals

In preparation for her duties as a working royal, Kate received much training from Buckingham Palace officials on appropriate **protocol** and **etiquette**. Her first public appearance with William as a married couple occurred on an official tour of Canada and the United States, from June 30 to July 10, 2011. They began the tour in Ottawa, Canada, where they attended Canada Day celebrations, at which Kate wore a red maple leaf hat, in honor of Canada's national symbol. They visited several Canadian regions before moving on to the United States. While in the US, they spent time in Los Angeles. Kate and William attended an elegant gala which included celebrity guests such as Jennifer Lopez and Nicole Kidman. The next day, they created art with children in a low-income area known as Skid Row. Overall, their first tour as husband and wife was considered a huge success.

Their last stop in Canada was in Calgary, Alberta, where they pressed a button to set off fireworks, signaling the start of the Calgary Stampede parade.

Stately Kate

Kate was considered immediately successful in her role as a working royal. The press was no longer calling her "Waity Katie." She was now "**Stately** Kate."

Kate's every fashion choice was closely watched. By now, something called "the Kate effect" had begun. Whenever she wears an outfit, it sells out in stores within hours. Kate doesn't always wear expensive designer labels. She often wears clothing that most people can afford, such as the $74 Zara dress she wore the day after her wedding.

On March 19, 2012, Kate gave her first public speech at the opening of The Treehouse, a children's hospice, or home for sick children. Kate wrote the speech herself.

She Said It

"What you do is inspirational…. The feelings you inspire, feelings of love and of hope, offer a chance to families to live a life they never thought could be possible."
—From Kate's first public speech, honoring the work of The Treehouse, March 19, 2012

Little Royals

After the wedding, the public began eagerly waiting for an announcement that Kate was carrying the next heir to the throne. This announcement finally came in December 2012. William and Kate's first child, George Alexander Louis, known as Prince George of Cambridge, was born on July 22, 2013. Their daughter, Charlotte Elizabeth Diana, known as Princess Charlotte of Cambridge, was born on May 2, 2015. Louis Arthur Charles, Kate and William's third child, known as Prince Louis of Cambridge, was born on April 23, 2018. All three children were born at St. Mary's Hospital in London, the same hospital where William had been born. During all three of her pregnancies, Kate suffered from an extreme form of morning sickness. She was placed on bed rest by her doctor for the first weeks of each pregnancy.

Kate's maternity fashion choices also contributed to "the Kate effect."

Modern Mom

Kate has put her photography skills to work and released some of her own shots of George and Charlotte to the public. In the past, official photos of the royal family were always taken by professional photographers. This is another example of Kate and William wanting to live their lives in a more natural and modern way than most royals have before.

In 2012, Kate also released some images she captured while on tour in Southeast Asia. In recognition of her skills, she was awarded an honorary membership to Britain's Royal Photographic Society, which is considered a very high honor.

Princess

Kate's daughter Princess Charlotte is called a princess, but Kate is not. Technically, Kate is a princess, but her official princess title is Princess William. Charlotte is the daughter of a prince, which is why she has the title before her own name.

An official family portrait on the day of Princess Charlotte's baptism

Giving Back

Kate is the **patron** of 13 charitable organizations. She chose her charities very carefully, to show her commitment to causes close to her heart. Many of the charities are for sick and vulnerable children and people battling addiction. In her role as patron, Kate shines a spotlight on each charity through speeches and appearances, helping to spread awareness and provide valuable media promotion.

Place2Be

Place2Be is one of the charities Kate patronizes. The organization provides emotional support to children dealing with violence at home, bullying, or other traumas in elementary and high schools across England.

Kate visits a primary school in her role as patron of the Place2Be charity

Making a Difference

The Royal Foundation of The Duke and Duchess of Cambridge and Prince Harry was set up by the three young royals to make a difference for causes that matter to them through investment and mentoring. Heads Together is one of their charitable endeavors. Kate, William, and Harry believe that talking openly about mental health issues, especially for children and teens, will help to end the **stigma** and raise awareness.

On October 10, 2017, on World Mental Health Day, Kate attended a reception at Buckingham Palace to pay tribute to mental health workers.

❝❝ She Said It ❞❞

"A child's mental health is just as important as their physical health and deserves the same quality of support. No one would feel embarrassed about seeking help for a child if they broke their arm, and we really should be equally ready to support a child coping with emotional difficulties."

—Kate speaking in a video message supporting Place2Be, released on February 16, 2015

Traveling Royals

The British royal family is partially funded by taxpayers. This angers some people, who feel the royal family has no real purpose. Others believe the royal family earns that money through their tireless charitable work and global promotion of British products and tourism, which greatly helps the economy. Many members of the royal family regularly travel around the world, especially to **commonwealth** countries.

In April 2014, Kate and William traveled with baby George to New Zealand and Australia, where one of the stops was a playdate for George with local children. In September 2016, the family traveled back to Canada, where George and Charlotte had a marvelous time at an outdoor children's party. On all their tours, George and Charlotte seem to be the true stars.

George and Charlotte got to check out some helicopters while visiting Poland and Germany with William and Kate in July 2017.

Hello, Mr. President

On April 22, 2016, George proved he could make headlines around the world while at home in his pajamas! Barack and Michelle Obama visited Kate, William, and the children at their home in Kensington Palace in London. Hearts around the world melted when a picture of George meeting the Obamas in his bathrobe was released.

Equality

A few years ago, male children were automatically in line for the crown even if they had an older sister. This changed in 2011. The British Parliament passed a law that females would now be equal to males for succession to the throne.

A New Era

Kate is enjoying a very busy 2018. In January, Charlotte started preschool. On April 23, Kate and William welcomed their third child, another son, Prince Louis. On May 19, the couple attended the wedding of Prince Harry and Meghan Markle. If Kate was considered a modern choice for a royal bride, Meghan is even more so—she is American, divorced, and **biracial**. Not very long ago, neither Kate nor Meghan would have been considered acceptable additions to the royal family. Both women have signaled the beginning of a more inclusive era in The Firm, making millions of people around the world very happy.

William and Kate leave St. Mary's Hospital holding Prince Louis. Kate's red dress is thought to be a tribute to Princess Diana, who wore a similar dress after Prince Harry's birth.

Kate and Meghan Markle attend the first annual Royal Foundation Forum held on February 28, 2018, in London, England.

Timeline

1982: Kate is born on January 9

1984: The Middleton family moves to Amman, Jordan, for two years

1986: Kate begins school at St Andrew's Prep

1987: Carole Middleton begins her at-home business, Party Pieces

1995: Kate begins school at Downe House

1996: Kate transfers to Marlborough College

2000: Kate begins her gap year, traveling to Florence and Chile

2001: Kate begins her studies at St Andrews University in Scotland and meets William

2002: Kate becomes one of William's roommates

2004: On April 1, the world learns about Kate and William's romance

2005: Kate and William graduate from St Andrews University

2007: Kate and William briefly break up

2010: The engagement of William and Kate is announced

2011: Kate and William marry at Westminster Abbey on April 29

2012: Kate delivers her first public speech at The Treehouse on March 19

2013: Prince George is born on July 22

2015: Princess Charlotte is born on May 2

2018: Prince Louis is born on April 23

Glossary

ambassador A representative or supporter of an organization

angora A fabric made from the hair of the angora goat or rabbit

biracial A member of two racial groups

charity An organization that raises money for people in need

class A system of ordering society based on social or economic status

commoner An ordinary person without rank or title

commonwealth An international association of states that are part of the British Empire

descendants A person's children and grandchildren

etiquette The accepted form of proper behavior

flight attendant A person who attends to airline passengers during a flight

flight dispatcher A person who plans flight paths

heave a line Throwing a rope from ship to shore

inclusive To not leave anyone out

Koran The sacred book of the Islamic religion

marine survey The inspection of vessels

mental health Psychological and emotional well-being

multicultural Several cultural groups in a society

paparazzi Freelance photographers who follow celebrities and take pictures to sell to publications

patron A person who gives financial or other support to an organization

prestigious To have a high status

promote To encourage interest in something

protocol An official set of rules

relatable Making people feel they understand you

stately Dignified in manner and appearance

stigma A feeling of disapproval many people have for something

trust fund A money fund set up by someone for someone else to use

working class The social group of people who work for wages

Find Out More

Books

Summers, Portia. *Kate Middleton: Duchess of Cambridge.* Junior Biographies Enslow Pub Inc., 2017.

Tieck, Sarah. *Kate Middleton: Real-Life Princess.* Big Buddy Books, 2012.

Websites

Check out this website for some fun activities and facts about the British royal family: www.activityvillage.co.uk/british-royal-family

The official website of Kate and William: www.dukeandduchessofcambridge.org

Visit this website to learn more about Heads Together, the charity focusing on mental health founded by Kate, William, and Harry: www.headstogether.org.uk

Index

About the Author

Petrice Custance is a writer and editor. She is happiest when she is walking her dogs, Bickey and Mickey, or getting pelted with snowballs by her nephews, Kyle and Tyler.